KING HORN

Edited by Michael Baldwin

Poems by Children
Illustrated by Michael Foreman

Michael Baldwin

KING HORN

*Poems written at Montòlieu
in old Languedoc
1969-81*

Routledge & Kegan Paul

London, Boston, Melbourne and Henley

First published in 1983
by Routledge & Kegan Paul plc
39 Store Street, London WC1E 7DD,
9 Park Street, Boston, Mass. 02108, USA,
296 Beaconsfield Parade, Middle Park,
Melbourne 3206, Australia, and
Broadway House, Newtown Road,
Henley-on-Thames, Oxon RG9 1EE

Set in 11 on 13pt Baskerville by
Rowland Phototypesetting Ltd, Bury St Edmunds, Suffolk
and printed in Great Britain by
St Edmundsbury Press, Bury St Edmunds, Suffolk

Library of Congress Cataloguing in Publication Data

Baldwin, Michael.
King Horn: poems written at Montolieu
in Old Languedoc, 1969–1981.
I. Title.
PR6052.A39K56   1983   821'.914   82-23068

ISBN 0-7100-9494-9

For Elizabeth and Pierre, their family and goats

The publication of this volume has been made possible by a
subsidy from the Arts Council of Great Britain, to whom
grateful acknowledgment is made.

Three of these poems are reprinted in revised form from my
selected poems *Buried God*. Six others were commissioned for
Thames TV pamphlets; others have appeared seriatim and at
random in magazines great and small, in anthologies, and in
memorial volumes to Eric Walter White, and the late Leonard
Clark. They were all written or drafted in Languedoc between
1969 and 1981 at

Domaine d'Arzens
par Montolieu

Contents

Author's note

Montolieu is a small town backed into the south flank of Black
Mountain in the Aude. It faces out to the Corbières and then the
Pyrenees across medieval vineyards and prehistoric ruins on
scrubby ridges. Slight but productive soil lies on top of ignaceous
rock and rich mineral deposits, including gold. The land around
is the natural habitat of the wild boar, the rough-legged buzzard
and the sand viper. Southwards the pools are fished by heron,
and then there are saltpans flaring with flamingoes. The people
are peasant farmers and related dependants on the grape. Their
chief recreations are hunting and sawing down telegraph poles.
Since their first tongue is Oc, or a midi French sweetened by Oc,
they see themselves as preyed upon by the Frankish North and
are prompt to cobble the wires on which the oppressor's language
hums. It is difficult sometimes to tell whether their uplifted
muzzles are blazing away at some unseen bird or the soft
underbelly of a police helicopter. They shoot without rancour and
their shot is so much pepper on the wind. None the less they are
an unforgiving people with a memory longer than that of even the
Irish. The centuries are all contemporary, kept vivid before them
in one of the five magic dialects of the troubadours; and in the
mirror of such a spell they still gaze in horror at the Albigensian
Crusade and the brutal subjugation of the South. In the
braincells of even the devoutest Catholics among them a myriad
Cathar ancestors are mummied up like bees, and when they
swarm to Heaven they intend to see that Simon de Montfort and
St Louis the Good – both of whom will undoubtedly have
travelled by a more circuitous route – are eternally locked out.

Juice

He was picking grey sticks for an April fire
When one curled and bit him. It clung to his arm
Short-toothed but tempered, pumping both glands
Till he unhooked his sleeve and bruised it under heel:
A viper, of course.
                         Here, in the South,
It's a serious thing, and this more than most
With a skullful of venom ripened all winter.
So he kicked it quite flat, first a trickle then a puddle,
Kick, kick, kick, enlarging his heart.

His arm bloated up, his belly, then his head
(They say that Snake is the old Wriggled Wisdom)
But that's not the point. It's a veinous poison:
You bleed in your joints, in your bowels, in your lungs
Till there's no blood to bleed, so recover or die.

Well, he lay in a trance half a week
And dreamed, he said after, how his bones were a tree
With cinders for apples, his limbs
Lagged in branches, his flesh growing teeth
Till drought sealed his arteries, the dead meat recovered
And his brain got better in a mindless way:
His tongue keeps dripping and he tastes of snake.

The woman on the next farm now keeps serum
For the sake of her children: she's a whole crop of vipers
With others in their belly. They come near the house
To gorge themselves on frogs in the runnel by the well.
You can smell their spurt of almond, hear their quick shadow.
One bit her dog.
                    He died in an hour,
Having less to dream of, just the juice and the coil,
Lapping water then milk, then the sadness of Nothing:
A big dog when bitten, but bigger when he died.

Unbroken Horses

I sleep in the crab's shadow
                among gnats
Under webs under dews whose liquidities mate:
Are these winds, are they frogs, or else snakes in a fly rustle?
I doze, but the grasses bite.

Then the horses straddle me,
Judith and Jubal, pushing the gate,
Him mounted on her in a landlocked shadow.
I wake in their cuddle, their but-butting

Over me, see as I huddle my fright
The moles on her belly, his foreskin
Like husk on a leek, a mummer's flayed stick,
While my thought comes apart in her nostril,

Four nostrils. I stumble away from their arch
And prod them a pole's length off from me,
Smell my way out of my dream
Still dazed by their turf-footed coupling

Which beats under bone to my ears
And browbeats me out of philosophy.
I notice the water on her gums,
His tail still frisking for flies

And find myself given to Gulliver's persuasion:
To be covered by covering horses,
For a little to black out my eyes
In the hump of a six-hoofed beast

Then this toothy grafting of heads
Is to grow out of truth with the landscape
Or find that lost time in the Orchard
When the harvest was bitter and danced.

Corbières

Hills above which Pyrenees float
Like ghosts in a nightshirt:

their lamppost of snows
cackles with frost after dark

and sputters till dawn
like gasfires breathing;

so far away their
avalanche whispers of ash

so nearly near
my eyes are put out

by a stone wind,
my nostrils sour

on a spring full of autumn
a summertime blueness of snows.

In the land of goats I read about goats,
How Buller demonstrating to the Boers
The efficacy of screw guns, shrapnel and things
Tethered twenty goats on a nearby hill
And blitzed them half an hour with a battery of guns

Then went to count corpses with fingers, toes, thumbs.

Bad luck for ballistics and worse for mathematics,
Failed to find twenty bleeding goats
Or even twenty bleating goats
Or any combination of dead or alive:
For the farmers' instruction found twenty-two
All all alive, alive alive oh,
One being gravid having dropped down twins.

A gunner myself once, I did the same thing
But that was with sheep,
The war quite another one, inside my head.

Rabbits and Stars

Last night there were more rabbits than stars,
Rabbits with glittering eyes, rabbits with teeth, rabbits with
                                                    milky tails,
Rabbits in constellations pulsing about the gorse,
Rabbits sedate in our headlights, slowfooting the frost on the
                                                    road.

Today, though the leaves are shining, the sun rises wet.
Today is a day for hunters. There are no stars.

Booted in mud, I am wading kneedeep,
My shins so nettled with weed they blister
Inside the bone, wear little runs of skin,
Little darns. I buoy up my ills

Being swollen by bubbles. These sugar
Such balms as are bagged in man's primal
Condition, three feet high in the tomb.
I look into toes: a distant dissolve

Down isinglass bone, my jellyflesh stung
To sullenness colder than white, my first foot
Slimmed by its long sea-burial,
Limper than string but fat with its own ghost.

From the loins long down is a fish
Foreshortened to shallowness; limbs waver
Their eels, could merge off, be sperm
In the trident religion, a seashot

Of spawn where waves slap in mackerel.
I take no crabs. My everything
Looser than nets lets everything through;
Hieroglyphs nose through my navel

To moon in the mirror, then magnet fish.
It is time to unbone, unravelling
My labyrinth. There are filaments
Of fool, certain foolish figments

So give away man. I could ebb far off,
My marrow disgorging its raddle
If it weren't for ill will,
A petulant gravitas

Which buckles on well
Like an old tried boot
Thickened by mud
But supple still on the foot.

Factory Fishermen at Bages

In an occish kind of coracle
They sit bone-faced

Attentive to eel traps

Doing like pond fishers
The wide world over
Apparently nothing

Muddlers of the net,
Fuddlers of the seine

Indolent with hooks

And trawling their brains
Say a fathom under
For lobsters, amphora

And Barbarossa's smile
Where it sails in its beard

Yet lifting up harvests
From the lukewarm tides.

Electric Storm

First thing up here the telephone fuses
Making a plastic bang in the corner
(There's a cut-out by the door, but the storm always beats us,
Striking its fist into magnetic rock):

You sit among sulphur for a second's shock
Then the lights go out, and you get red ears
Supposing you'd been phoning when the lightning struck,
Your skull now stinking in the fish-smell of the phone.

So you strike two lamps and a priest-faced candle,
But what need of light? The sky switches on,
Switches off, and then settles down to a noon-bright flicker.
You can read a whole sentence at the time

With subordinate clauses, snatch a biblical verse,
Translate from the French.
                              Or else close your eyes
And listen to the long-tailed water
Come sliming in off the hills and grizzle its way

Through the silences under the field,
The rat's nest under the hearth,
The cellarage under each stone
Where it deepens into the world.

There are six sticks here, drying out slowly
To kindle a brain in the fire, and warm up some wits.
Till they kindle we're short of a flame,
Standing fat when thin, sitting thin when fat
But mostwise like skeletons walking, in great trances walking
Like hedgehogs in bigoted lines, and breathing the straw in our
                                                                    lungs,
All the faggots and thistles and hurdles, but coughing like cats.
It is better up in that shed where the beasts push meat against
                                                                    meat
Dropping birth in a rumour of cud, vibrations of fiery hay;
Up there or that hut where he kept her young body in stones,
A year and a day in hot stones
To build up his blood and grow a sweet fig-tree or prickle.

Alaric

Sun fills the helmet.
Ice melts. The warrior
Blows snow from his teeth
Howls once like a wolf

Then challenges Frost.
Over ten hills
Icicles chatter.
Ghosts clatter down

With ox-horn for shield
And fangs on a stick.
He grins and holds back
Their white rush,

Then settles the land
With thorn rake or plough
Made of flint. He plants
Only gristle, Roman eyes, Roman bones.

There are no tracks yet,
Just the rivers in rut
While Old Gods move
On the cattlepath

Leaving no signs
But kicked-out stones
Whose springs chuckle harvest
After six dry moons.

When rains come
The sky out of its importance
Tips all its nearer meaning
Changing the limits, changing the surface limits.

Rivers may swallow their banks
But not too often. Houses become unfixed
But never here, and then by the swirl of earth
More than weirs of slurry.

The sky is a single Ocean.
The Po comes down in the Mississippi
But still no moccasin swim
Through the upstairs window;

When cellars flood
The scale is weighed with the rat,
Is the prey of uncertain fish
In their downstairs midnight.

So when rains come
They come on to kapok dogs,
Onto decent cockerel,
Ducks bone clean on midsummer mud

Now muttering wet; they come
Onto well caulked unwilling pigs,
Incensing a snot-ulcered mountain of bucks
To parabolas of ecstasy

And only the fly-headed herds,
Wearers all day of the riddled leather
Wince at the peck peck of water
Rinsing their pus, the lens on their craters of pus;

And if worms gape up by the acre
Our carrion are in hiding.

At the moment of storm, hill storm, things
Rest exact. A whiteness touches the land,
Absorbs its green. Trees lock
To nearly earth, soil thins in upwardness

Until there is land in the sky,
An alternative magnet, sucking up atoms,
Stretching the mirror. Grass grows out long
Into halos of grass, bushy gas

And cattle who'd lie down for rain
Stand to chew. Some eat in air.
In the closeness that comes from no noise
You hear the soft flight of their tongues

And hoofs overhead. The cloud
Is a worm on the neck, is a trickle of clod
Is a white root of green with the damp dripping out of it,
A weight in the marrow of the ear, an enormous cud,

Then the stillness moves, goes treading about
As the skyline tightens its jaws
And the weather comes, trees whirl like waterspouts,
The hills start to dump their stones.

The Wind

is emptying its boxes
it is folding little pieces of glass
it is chewing its thistle

upstairs in the blackstone hill
where tonight is splitting

He came out early, fog early
Gathering juniper berries
And what they best cook with, snails.

Picking the blue of berries,
The midnight nostrils of snails,
He saw what hangs beyond berries,
He found what crawls beneath snails:

The egotrip of the moon,
The pocky abeyance.

Albert

Smelling of man in the Old Orchard
Where no apples, no figs, no pears
Only vines, cobbled tiny, lift their heads like asps
And dribble sappy sweatdrops,
Smelling of man which is mostly of tooth

You plant yourself a hoe,
Make slogans with your sickle
And pretend to shorten flints
But only pretend: a flint has its traditions,
A fossil its politics

Like you in your long-bollocked trousers,
A man with the backside of a cow and a pocketful of udder
Who can stride into this hill
Which is made of three trees and turn into a mirage
Smelling of green clay, smelling of your tooth.

The Sheba Goat

Arthritic, her flint milk
Dried to a piddle of mica
Like a stone run out of spark,

She nibbles here in mid-season
(Only her second in milk)
With her bone noise all gone brittle,
Her footfall chalky with pain.

Sometime this afternoon
At the end of our slow siesta
The hammer, the blade in the throat:
Already she circles, waiting,
Held by a needless chain.

At least she's an oily coat,
Too lush for her vigil here –
It will do for a chair-backed woman.
I see her, waiting to die,
And think of my mother's death

Afflicted in walking like this
But browsing from room to room
In similar parchment process

Disdaining the draughts of her chair,
Not kibing once at her chain.

Kingdom

On the one civil bowl
To the west side of Black Mountain
I sit from the sun
And consider the sun-dust on my feet.

Sometimes a snake pokes its nose
Down the airing-pipe: it might be a frog
(A poet has licence, but not to lie),
Something with a tip of reptilian intelligence.
I hit it on the snout in the shadow of my leg
With a quickly rolled page of *La Dépêche*
And blur out of sleep. Suppose it returns
Now I've run out of paper? Shall I hit it with my fist
Or amaze it with my shadow? Or let it in its turn
Take possession of the bowl?
A Man, I know, must fight for possession;
A Man, I know, is King in his Kingdom
And even the Lion and the Unicorn,
The cerebral Lion and the dreamy Unicorn,
Even the mud-loined earth-fastened Bull
Must bow down to Man who holds the key to the Kingdom.
And this is my Kingdom. I trust I have the key.

But a Snake, simple Snake who was first in the Garden,
Or possibly a frog, who may or may not have a snake behind him
in the pipe
(And if so will soon be in the pipe of the Snake)
Surely this Snake or this Frog
May have access to my squatting shade,
The only Summer shade
On the west side of Black Mountain?
They do not threaten me;
Nor threaten one member of the staff of *La Dépêche*.
I have them to consider, I have it to consider,
A certain summer harmony well shaded from the sun
On the hot side of Black Mountain
With the keys of my Kingdom
While the dust rains on my feet.

Watching three cats on the lawn,
One watching a bird, one watching the watching,
One eating a grasshopper, I saw
Summer dwindle because of them,
Moths, mice, birds, little glints of wind:
They had killed them all, not disdainfully,
And eaten them. Even the doorstep toad
Swallowed last year by the snake
And kicked by Pierre's boot up again
Bewildered from the vomit of the snake,
Even that was gone, and the snake was gone;
Neither snake to toad nor boot to snake
Having been to the other's detriment
Till the cats had come, drawing their week-old spit
From a dead mother, suckled on ghost's milk,
Ghost's then goats' on a fingernail,
Mouse–faced howling no noise and growing
Stick–bodied, like daylight owls gaping their silences.

Watching three cats on the hot lawn,
Three full-grown hunting cats,
One eating a bird, one licking up ants,
One mantissing air with its paws,
All watching the watching

I felt claws freckle my back,
I felt the sun purr at my back.

Last night ago from my windowsill
Catface nosed in. Between each wing ear
The simplistic eyes, the thought-rays of hair.
A three-quarter moon made the landscape purr

Blurring my sleep in its glazed cradle
Till a bloodbeat took it. I fell
Into now, as snipped up by bill,
Hooked high by claw, it cat-hissed

A whole hill off, squawling through airs
In my unopened eye that saucied its kill.
I followed through dreams till its death spattered,
Woke as its screech hinged shut.

So large a cat. The three-quarter moon
Scarcely inched. A cold boil of crickets
Bubbled the outside grass, not pogoing
High, not brushed up by panic,

No gust to say how it went, whether
Fox, or by nightstrike, some huge wing
Or the flapped away mind of the world,
It was gone. I spent starlight looking.

At dawn, it left slops of bread,
And at milking, the hot smoke of milk.
The others are here, looking smaller now
Close to the house with their pride sucked out,

While I walk, calling to shades. From stones
I assemble its eyes, from leavings
The prick of its ears; but no flesh follows
And rabbits come up on the lawn, and snakes

Unmolested snakes, with the slowness of glass
To lie stiff out, uninteresting as carrots.

When the Night Shriek howls, you are safe, little vole,
Little mouse, little frog, little fang. It's when
The keening stops that the great claws fall
Through their cloudbase of feathers. Men

Found the same with that Flying Bomb:
When it went scolding on with its ram-lag and sputter
The whole fragile tribe could wait with aplomb.

When its bragging stopped, the silence was utter.

Dawn Squirrel

There, beyond the tap-tap of wind, the paw-tip on the pane,
The daft little nuzzle of a nose more mute
Than the pigeons' knock knock, softer again
Than the sparrows' scurry: squirrel is here

Begging for indulgences a minute after dawn,
Licking at his nose's smear, peering with one-way eye
At the unglued feather of the moon blowing in from the sill,
Leering us awake, sneering at a cat too dark for eyes

As the window opens and he grendels in
Grinning through a tickertape of flowers
And chippering his teeth till the nuts fall down,
Nuts without salt from cellophane

While he sits on a pool of sleep in a mirror
And with sappy feet, sticky
With the sweat of trees, the balsamum of dawn,
Disfigurement of birds, turns it to a puddle

To say he was here. He was never here:
He was only the trees blowing in, and these
Are the husks of stars; there were never nuts,
And never a squirrel. A rat perhaps,

A rat shall we say with lopsided brain
And a peacock's tail? I can see his shit.

I can eat you, little beast, little bird;
I can empty your brain of religion,
Your footfall of genesis and guile,
I can eat you down to your heartbeat,
I can eat you and not blaspheme.

But when I see men waste meat
I think of you romping in fur,
Your last icarian feather.
If the bone's not clean on the plate
I wonder what God lies there.

The Ritual

That morning I saw his soft eyes,
His hide like dried grass,
As he stalled there, waiting for death.

That evening I ate him,
Ate him all up,
All the love in its tenderloin,

Licking his sticks, their immaculate hinge,
The bilberry wine, the lungs in their glade,
And lastly his eyes. I ate him all up.

His brain smelled like mine, full of poems.
Now my blood is like his, growing thin.

Fly Wind

The wind, this last wind, pushed everything over:
Trees starting forth at the hinge, diagonals of birds –
Even a stone flicked straight into air blew ten feet sideways –
Slates, stooks, men. But it never moved a fly.

So I've come to consider the world of the fly
Immobile on the back of the mobile world,
Eating its meat, goggling its stained-glass faeces,
Skubaring the bowels, spaceman from the planet of Rot

Spreading more manure weight for weight
Than a ploughboy carries on his boot
Or his spaded wheel. Light, but glued into air
Stiller than a bee, seeing more moons than the owl

And switching on wings with more cheeky importance
Than tu-whit-tu-woo, then winching down
From his rotors of mica through the slap-clap of hands
To drill little holes in your patchwork sleep.

He'll go helicoptering over the room and sticky the ceiling
With sometimes a stipple of your blood
A balderdash of semen. You dream on, three to a cot
And meanwhile he's listening to your eyeball,

Waxing in your brain, while his simultaneous friends
Are exploding the hide of your untinned bull
And blowing cans with a recipe of mildew
In spite of your spiders, your cool dream of frogs.

You wait for the quarter of the moon that will bring
A holier wind, which will not draw him off
But in which he'll vanish, a deft itch at the time.
Meanwhile snap him in your mouth: he tastes like pepper

Or the nostrils of a saint. Snap him in your mouth.
The moon whirs slowly. The mind is full of mouths.

Snakes in the Salt Pans at Gruissan

On crab days south in the lake
The snakes rise slowly, picking for air,
Sometimes a foot, sometimes three feet long,
But slim enough still to have hiss breath:

Spiralling, tail-tipped in slime
(The longer the snake the deeper its water)
So tentative they come, a liquoring upness
Of the lickerish essence, a silence at the time

Smokesignalling sunwards from creation's floor
Tornadoing slow around hollow muscle –
Yet a delicate rise as the old saints rise
Or man on his belly-thread of prayer –

For a brief gulp at heaven. Then
Sink through their circle like pouring a coin;
Some who are taller than the reeds
Can lick black sunshine by the gull's minute

Till miracles collapse. These,
Breathless with air, bask on discomfort
Lying then lifting, sometimes all day
Before soothing shorewards to their thumb-hole in the fen

Swallowing as they slide among bubble-gum frogs
And panicking the land with their influx of wisdom.
Some dry inside the gap that bore the Tree;
Some flay into sunset under salty wings.

Two Oil Lamps

(fashioned from artillery projectiles)

All over these hills, the old 75s,
Snouting magnetic rock or rusting in grasses –
Snubs of grey iron in a green copper garter
Scored by the bore, and crusted in salt –
Convert into cruets, or bases for lamps.

One might go off in your hands even now,
Leaving them full of their own broken branches,
But that's not likely, fifty years from the War
And the Range gone elsewhere,
To the tundra tofts or the South Pacific.

Yet thunder strolls on these hills
And sometimes lightning will fire one
To shower a sheltering goatboy in fragments.
I had one shot at me once: it's a dangerous gun
But the lightning alone does better.

Meanwhile we perch our lamps into sills
And watch the St Elmo's fire on our cruets,
While the flocks outside are riddled by storm,
Drilled by the outbursting stars
And broken all night by the thunder's rolling.

Heron at Gruissan

I know the age of that heron:
It is ancient as incest, has the pedigree of stone
And for a million years it has practised its hunger
Which it learned from the volcano, to guzzle the lake.

I think I cannot hear it, and yet I see it utter
A mud-smack of syllables on the dry side of time.
If I listen to anything I am listening to nails,
Nails without hammers, nails that sink like worms

Nails driven in by the light of their echoes,
Nails are they nails it will mutter tomorrow,
Nails in the mind, quintessential nails;
I come to offer nails for the shingle is a hammer

As that stilt-lipped long-legged relative of cranes
Stammers into flight, meccanoing its way across the lake
Which is frothing with eels. These it eggs into its beak
Then graceless in indolence gargles on spawn.

Flamingoes at Gruissan

And then the flamingoes
                         always since always there
At the shingled end of the lake
In a daylong sunset of colour
Paddling a shore which is ten thousand years
                                     of their petals,
A steepening hatchback of shells:

Where the beach stays wet, where the lake
Is a sliminess of mud, they move on slowly
Picking up stick legs slowly, then ordering them slow in the silt,
So big a bird, yet disturbing nothing

As dunking dumbly, gossiping eels
They go where the shoreline glimmers with fish
                         and their own hot metals.

Sometimes they up and fly shallow away,
Doing more to water from the air
In their long billow over, in their gust of ripples
Than in wading ever

And leaving their colour on the shale
In a downfall of feathers
                         that stutter the eye
Like that first bruise of light
When the sun goes missing.

So What Can I Do with her Bucket?

Somewhere a little way south Leonardo
Wrote of the reflex of water,
The molecular brickwork of waves.
He preferred his moisture humped up in oceans,
The mirrors changing places in the big seas building.
It took a silly Englishman, Traherne, to discover
There was magic tucked under the corner of a puddle,
Sheep, sky, men in a thumbnail of spit.

So what can I do with her bucket,
Full of little water but shimmering with nails?
She is nailing my floorboards with splashes
Like a sow's tears.

Buzz

No wind. There will be flies today.
The sun on the cornhill is wild as a hoop.

Look at Albert there, his body beetled at harvest,
And Anna with cracked out eyes come bluebottling up the hill

And the little old woman next door already a wasp.

Rain Gauge on Cinder Mountain

Clearing the pluviometer,
gauging the depth of rain
the imminence of snow
the miraculous dew

I come close to see
dead flies in a pyramid
wasps in a turk tower
a beetling peabug's head

a whole day of heaven
compressed to a snail's slime
an imperial frog's vomit
an old cac

as if today
like the day before today
and before yesterday
we had dry rain

a bone-dry deciduence
on a drystone land,
a reading of crystal
a cistern of soul's juice.

Yet where can I tell
in what graticule of what prism
how two-legged cinders crawl
skywards on white wings

Les Bonshommes lighter than ash
their wisdoms aflicker
as flaring their nostril
they rain souls upwards?

Where can I catch
their truths in a funnel?
Unless at Toulon
where under a moat

then under a toad stone
wearing his brains
in his belt of brains
squats Simon de Montfort

in dung like a radish
still burning bones
and baking dry rain
in the bonfire sun.

Netting Snakes in the Sea Pans at Gruissan

They swim with fuddled pulse, just as pond snakes swim
Save for upward undulations that concur
With the crockery of waves, demurring to a ripple
Flutter-backed, till their wake's a wicker muddle

Or their pattern meets your shadow so they curl
And furl their wriggle, sink to silt beneath the glass,
Fur themselves like worms in particles of stillness
Until again they see you or sense your shady tread

Then dart off as on land, with their old
Grassnake wiggle perhaps a little languid
In this stiffer dimension. You can seek them
In its syrup as they ferment through the mud

And snatch them into air. They rasp stalk-throated
But flap about the hand less muscular than eels
And, most unlike an eel, examine your eye
While testing its experience with a sputter of the tongue

Still hissing as through straw, then bite out in panic.
You have to use your hands, they're quick
From a net, so it's fingers not string
Or they'll plop back through their meshes

Uplifting gouts of darkness, a blurred ink bush
From the smoke of the sand; and somewhere the Original
Of Serpent is sliding round your toes
To alarm you out of giggles. Greensnakes, of course,

Smoothsnakes at most, playing plastic games
In the grass-green water. Yet vipers do it too
And sometimes you approach one that will coil
And offer strike. It would do it to a dog,

It would do it to a God, so why not you
With your sun-bellied shadow splashing goose-footed?
These are easier to net and easier to lift
Since they dizzy with height

So cling to what's nearest, even string. You swing them
Through the seashine giddily compliant –
Thus have your snake, and everyone applauds.
The trouble comes later when it drops back into water:

Again the smoky plume, the dense branch of silt.
The old dance is on, the toes very ticklish
As the snake becomes several in several directions
Through all the known dimensions and some not known.

If your mind lacks a declension, if you baulk
At too much time or the ten small facts
That swallow you, then fish a snake in water,
A viper say in water becoming cloudy water

And you up to your waist in worry grown opaque –
An allegory of my kind of living
Which is made up of avoidance
Though stops short of flight.

[41]

Upwind

Upwind, a pony shaking her nostrils out,
Unfolding them fleshy like cyclamen,
Has halted my spider pen
And brought me the morning in:
The children have salt-white hair,
There is glass glint under the vines
And a lizard fetching flies from an opened tin
(Or at least flies form and disappear
And the lizard is accurately there)
And somewhere on the summer of the air
Someone does something with a saw
More musical than logging:
All because a pony shakes her nostrils out,
Discovering a tremble in the dust
And goes running, running.

Heat

Horses and far off the streams stink.
Goats grow a backbind of bark, scratch against trees;
The does fratchet. Wasps eat holes in the sun,
Hooves pin the breeze, and then dung

In an anchored-down freight of stale straw.
Last night the rain flew in song, and I followed its graph
Till the gun stopped it. Where wings went blinking
Beaks hang on sticks, there's a glue of feathers

Too stiff for each draughting of goats
As they turn and then turn in some feeble antic,
Nose up, then tail up in heat
Or hotly in milk, cosmetically shitting.

My eyes glaze on shale, there is haze on the hills
So I study these goats, the five-month-old does
Then the dirty girls chewing my sleeve
Which smells of the buck or is buckish with cheese,

Little does, little wives, little sproutings of wisdom
Until under gliders of horn
Come the grandmother goats, great belles dames
With cobbles in their eye and a lick of braille

Surrounding me now, tilting their heat,
Concentrically chewing and butting and coughing,
Choking their feed to the cud's rhythm
And bandying hocks round their udders.

Here they are truly hot,
Babooning their monkeyish fruit –
Milk in a pot of lard
Like Buddha between their legs,

Dripping such staling of teat
On blue clay and all over heaven,
And eating up cordite and truffles
Or hair from a Goth's bone face.

The Tribe of Hot

When birds delirious for water
Craze into thickets, men sit by the pool
And not by the thorn
(The pool was the women's place
Till mud cracked its puddle).
The women, grain-footed indoors,
Grainfooted, glass-jointed, gravel-boned,
Move their shadows in a coolness thick as lint
Smelling wine, dried berries, salted meat
Among puncheons stone-cold as sweat
Disdaining the man talk, the egg-whites of spit
That gather undissolved on the dry skin of the pool:

They find none the less
No gossip indoors, cannot think
Even babytalk so heavy is the light,
Even babytalk to babies or foottalk to cats
Or how They'll-not-say-his-name

Digs that gypsy girl's bottom every night into the hill
From her tail striking sparks
And bringing us this heat
In which our baked sweetmeats curdle like brains.

Day of light airs,
Day of the grass-rake:
God's indigo arm
On my silly shoulder

I hear the tractor start
And then fail to start,
See the leaf fall twice
From the same twig in heaven.

I daresay I am blessed.
I dare say I am blessed.
I avoid one ant
While the leaf falls again;

The tractor not starting
Does duty in silence,
Is a new form of silence,
It helps the furled furrow

Shake itself open
Then the field shake open,
The leaf fall again
Because of one ant

Because of light airs
There's a tulip in the grass-rake
Because of God's arm
On my silly shoulder

I dare say I am blessed
I daresay I am blessed

[46]

The Fish are Retrograde

The fish grumble close under weed
And breathe out pop pop:
Do they yearn for the Eighteenth Century Tradition?

A greater backwash of calm
From the pendant weir?

Rousseau could not fish.
Voltaire did not fish,
Having lost his twine in intelligent women.

I sit here through two quarts of wine.
The fish are not reading their Rousseau,
Do not mention Voltaire.

The Second Goat Poem

for Jojo

His bones snap like trees;
He has got tree bones,
Coral brains, horns of arthritic rock
To sparkle his pyromanic fantasy:
Somewhere his midsummer tongue
Sets the gorse alight
And this smoking dawn
Is shammed by his tinder hide
As he ambles the garrigue –
A wit from the bestiary of night

Walking, as goats walk, on air
Disdaining little marbles of dew
And treading on the green exhalations
If treading at all, yet goatishly tangible
Once twilight ends, with himself the limit
And surrounding me time to time with grins –
Dandelion eater of the marble hills,
Gossiper of snot, chewing his luck
In the dwindle of a starhole
And leaving little tracks, little signs
On the wet world blanket:
There! I hear him cough
His dribble of renewal.
He keeps himself moist
Now the branches are his lungs.

He gives his little thimbleful of milk
And the flock runs on milk,
Three hundred teats all gone spunky
At one little prod from his nail –
But that was last year, with his mind on nothing.

Now he is serious.
He has gone to be dead,
To be a thighbone and a haunch
And a bearded coat
And the glue from his hoof.

His horns are discardable
(Although they outstand both buffalo and elk)
Being three-quarter sawn
Since he broke off a tip on the Chief of Police.

I sniff him as he heads along the herd,
His forehead still sprouting genealogies,
The small bucks lording in his shade.
When I die, I am useless.
When the Chief of Police dies, he will be
A name on a plaque. Jojo

Has many plaques. Is nailed
Three times above the door,
Is succulent and edible,
And outside, under the hammering leaves,
His wickednesses run.

Gunsmen

Blueskinned with good morning
gunsmen front the breeze,
roll up rabbit carpets,
sieve blood through cut-glass trees

and all day long they dandle
the dead meat in their smile.
I smell them. They go walking
their death's concentric mile.

No ghost goes on before them;
no thing stays live behind,
no fin, no fluff, no feather
in the long smear of their mind.

Save One who walks there lonely
and both ways of the breeze
rolls up no rabbit carpets
nor sieves the blood of trees:

That Gunsman dreams of nothing,
no lightnings leave his head;
his flesh glares down no shadow,
he roves on weightless tread.

Butterflies fumble through him,
Birds unwise his hair
and cobwebs blind his barrel
to nest and set and lair:

and, gunsmen, he kills nothing
but gives the dead flesh back,
walking the broken pastures
with tomorrow in his sack.

I'm only digging your garden, little snake,
So please hiss off. This centre is mine
And I give it to cucumber. I need it for food.
Leave me in the centre with worms in my salad
And make yourself free in the wall,
Make free with the hole in the wall . . .

He would come and go. She would come and go.
It is hard save for snakes to be sure about snakes.
Is it male or female? Was it here? Is it gone?
A snake is very wise. It is right to be uncertain.

Every man should have a snake in his garden,
Try to chase it out, then keep on one side.
It will keep him on tiptoe
Or on stilts as for prayer.
He will learn to heed shadow. He will come to value salad.

Also he will use his own sweat for perfume.
Snakes grow used to familiar smells
And never bite a friend unless pressed
As Cleopatra knows, that or else sat upon.

They don't strike at friends, but there might be an Enemy
Whose pride you want bitten,
An Enemy, or woman, or particular friend;
And a gumful of venom is sovereign for pride

So distant from doctors, so far gone in wine.

Presumably a Starling

It lay crushed up, one-eyed,
A too-blooded bit of the pylon's fruit
Like a winged eggshell,
And all of it so muddied, so maimed
I could not tell it what it was
As it lay its livings in my hand –
Somewhere in size between a sparrow and an eagle

With a fixed steady pipe, a protest not at pain
But beseeching the beak-faced moon of its mother
To beam into its brain
Say comfort's last maggot.

I did what I could – in my twigs, in my bones
In a box, with a wet pipette,
While it went on piping, sweet-living mess,
For one more day.

In the morning it had died, this little all bird
Somewhere in size between a sparrow and an eagle,
And outside in the lattices of light
The usual feathered particles were singing.

Ninetieth Goat Poem

Goats sneezing, goats coughing, goats farting,
Goats pissing, all with a certain discretion
Under the sago sky, the bag-pudding sun
Which is white with their steam, though bloodshot with wine.

Ah, Nanny, I reverence discretion,
Ah, Billy, I reverence discretion.
The little goat joins me in reverence.
We rustle our lip. We concur.

As I sip, let me put you a question
(I have done my best with the trees,
I have fingered the book of the stones
So, who, save you, is my oracle?):

Why in this world baked from sweetmeats
Why does your Holiness prefer
To feast upon tinder? Do you nibble dreams
From the thistle's cinder, the lightning's bread?

Is it from the scroll overhead
With your mouthful of apples and nails
That you find a quick message in thorns?
Or your magic corner of the zodiac?

The Sixth Age

At sixty, man becomes his animal:
That one next door who ferretted the womb
With snarly eyes and tore its bark to shreds,
Who sucked his thumb and drank the nipple up,

Well, he unlocked the wall.
                       He's back again
Endlessly catching snails, which breed and then escape –
Or keeps them rashly in his mushroom pot
Spoiling midmorning omelettes by the score;

He shoots at birds and only hits the skies,
Or stalks a boar and kills the mountainside;
Yet, slowly now, he's firmer on firm legs
And closer to the ground.
                     At dawn, with broken gun

He stands quite still among the junipers,
The birdsong breaks inside him
And his skull
Is warm with waiting like a woman's hole.

On a gallows of straw
Tonight they hung Silence:

A fifteen foot drop
Cut his white turds in half
And shed liquid neckbone
The length of his leg.

I heard the stars thud.

When she took up and died
No-one was left
To share out the hurt
So I write myself this letter
Consoling her grief.

Montségur

Certain only of bones –
those fifteen faults in the skin

the footbones bigger than feet
the kneebones broader than knees
the wishbones taller than towers
the leg like a telescope aimed
into pole bones under the groin
the woman bone's marrowless grin
the man bone's unmade shape
like a stab turned inside out,
the juicebone of the brain –
I am sure there is beauty's bone
as under this ugliness
bellybones stuffed with leaves,
bodybones dredged with glass
and rustle bones when we kiss
gutsing our boneless eyes

Somewhere a bird, not a folded lung,
Somewhere a bird neither real nor other
But a pattern flown in from the white side of night,
Somewhere a bird kills the wriggling marrow
And perching on one last branch of the bone

Is someone's death. It is someone's death
Calling crac crac in the dawn,
Calling come out to the Goddess of Claws
We shall worship each other in an uplift of feathers.

It is someone's death, I know the tune
Looking at my body lying parchment white
In its scrawl of riddles, I know the tune
In the rhythm of your flesh as it writhes
On the harvest of your sleep in whose is the beak?
It is someone's death being broken to chaff
In a mirror of seeds, and I hear it again

Somewhere a bird neither real nor other
Somewhere a bird kill the wriggling marrow
Somewhere a bird, not a folded lung.

Catching Snakes in the Wall

I was looking for little ones,
They had all been small,
Slowworm size, no bigger round
                    than a baby's finger;
So when the big one came
From out of a smallness deep in the wall
A wrist-sized inch at the time
Pouring into himself and along himself,
Building first a head with eyes straight forward,
Putting questions in front with his split-faced tongue
I was not afraid. To move
From his path would invite confusion:
Besides, he kept his mouth almost closed,
His fangs hinged shut.
                    Yet he must have known
My aroma was there as he grew into lengths
And tasted my presence on his tongue,
All my brain's warmth, and the rodent at my groin,
But kept himself going.
                    I still did not move.
He still did not turn, but came straight through me
Like a conjuror's sword or that old sorcerer's
Stick in the desert, coming stomach high
                    as I crouched
But straight off the wall, rupturing my mind,
Eye into eye like a folding of telescopes,
Merging each to each in a shuffled pack of ghosts.

Now I feast on little snakes, the big one
Never seen again, having come once from the void
And entered my shadow.

Pig Fruit

She built her first nest in grass, yellow grass
                   to match her wide ears,
And lay in a trough of dust, belly deep,
The nest itself lined with a few gorse roots
Torn quick with one foot which now lightly bled
On this quaver of ants.
                  Thus betrayed, and betrayed
By the swarming of flies, and a wasp more greedy for blood
Than melon or muscat, she twittered an uncovered ear
And screamed once sharp, contracting the Ten Acre Gorse.

This I heard, and on stockinged feet unmindful of snakes
Came up to her.
              Gorse: no harm to her half-inch hide.
Dust: no harm to the promised blood. What else could she choose
But gorse or magnetic rock, which now from under this gorse
Injected its filings?
             Round at her uncovered end
Like the passage of slime, or fruit from a vintner's anvil,
The first piglet fell, its mouth snailed-up in a bubble of living,

Its cry like a hold in Time.
              I looked
                 Look at man-pig now,
Prehistoric cousin from the echoing loins
With only its beak-face less than human,
And this so close to a three-month foetus
It might be homunculus
Fussed out of wax from a wizard's thigh:

One after one they fell, little rubber pigs,
While onlookers came, other men, other pigs
And watched for creation's oozings, brushed away flies,
Set a hurdle of straw against winds

Then clustering flesh, both pigs' flesh and man's,
While they lay, dirt-still, on a land
Rolling halfway to shade and turning its back on them:

In spite of their forced-open mouths, their pulse-steady cry,
They were hairless, born early with transparent skin,
Too lidded their eye, and the sow's dugs milkless.

So then, in a cold change of wind
From the top of Pic du Nore, from the summit of clouds,
                              from the ice-tip of Canegou
The moment passed through,
Piercing pigskin then bales, then straw-blooded men,
Till it reached them with dying.

We lifted rubber handfuls, blew air in their mouths,
Tucked them under shirts and ran rock-footed
Over hectares of iron
To the smoke-filled house and a warm kitchen table
Then watched as one by one, just as easy as living
They went slipping through to another place in time,
Turning back to mother lard,
Efting out in fleshy drippings,
Leaving life signs only
In each elephant snout, or the set of volish paws.

Long minutes later, in wine, I tasted their saline breath,
Their mother's brack in my mouth.
Sow's blood tainted my shirt and writhed in my belly's pulse.
Stripping, I found her lees, clogged hard in the scab of my navel.
Hosed at the outside tap, I saw that my friend, the farmer,
Having frozen one death for the vet,
Was throwing out the rest to the dogs.

There, quite close to the pump,
Surrounded by slime and by suds,
Eleven pigs dangled on brier,
Twitched between winds
Or lay like mushrooms on mixen

While the farmhouse dogs
And the hamlet dogs
And the village dogs,
Their stale cry bringing up dogs,

Chewed with unanxious jaws
To the lifeless heart of my dream.

Memorial to a Magic Lady

I have to report
      what her daughter reports
That somewhere at the middle of the century
Her body hole turned itself inside out.

She would walk with it trailing by the knee
Though masked by her grandmother skirt,
Like a buffalo with unshed afterbirth,
A kind of red rubber bedtime bottle into which
The pressures of her aging ebbed and flowed.

This did not diminish her gravitas,
Nor in her two peasant languages her wit;
Nor did her eighty year stoop
That bent her back forward an inch each year
Until it paralleled the ground.
'If I lifted my skirt behind,' she would say,
'You would see how like I am to a cow!'
(Not mentioning 'vache', but a mellower word in Oc)
'When my knuckles tap on the ground I'll be scared
That buckgoat Jojo'll give me a poke!'
(Being vulgar perhaps, but scarcely uncouth in Oc;
Not mentioning scared, not exactly, either,
But claiming an instinct, also in Oc)

About peasant lore she taught me a lot
Five minutes at the time, five minutes a year –
Speaking high-horned words to walk through my poems
Or nibble at thorns in the oxide hills.

These last ten years
Nature played a trick through the bugle of her body
For the sake of her family, good for her wit.
She would eat ten labourers'
Rations in a day, taking each meal a pack of bread and meat
Then stack it away with headlong hunger
Through the toothless vowel of her mouth
As if she carried quins or were feeding a grave
As she was in a sense

Since her old body rattled with the usual diseases –
Dangerous when awake, and ah when asleep
In that boarded room where three families slept
A nightly occupation. The pig, even he
In the cupboard complained.

She died of a stroke just after breakfast
While sniggering her gums round a fresh bowl of chocolate
Tasting bitterly indelible of goat.
She sat on her hard wooden chair and it took
For two good reasons lots of hands to lift her,
A great belle dame communally mourned
Even more widely than a curé or a witch.

I was not there when she died,
When my mother died,
When my grandmother died.

When any woman dies that I greatly care for
Chance has me walking unknowing on the hills.

The Return

Morning. Allover spider cold.
A dog's bark like leather on glass.

I get up, hearing her walk
With her worn-heeled shuffle on the cob,
Her tappit up-and-down with her stick, just the way it is.

One cough. More breath than cough
But audible as dawn, audible as leaves when spiders are:
Carbon, I suppose, in the cylinder –
She always stitched close to a candle-flame –

Then call good day, but remember she's dead,
Three weeks' dead though loud in the fog.
Her son new-awake next door
Is now moaning clear,
Her son and her man-voiced daughter-in-law.

Well, it took ninety years to bury her
So's she's bound to be about a bit
On days when there's help in the air

And then that first morning when they milk the vines.

We must watch for her then if we pickle a pig.

Taurean Dawn

I wake before summer dawn.
It is the Bull's time, the Bull's hour
Stagnant with tongue, slippery with marrow.
Small skulls mushroom underfoot,
Become snails. Here fox, here fungus,
Here rabbit, the lost brittle of a star.

There are small grits up.
The wind glistens
Blowing from a sense behind the sun.
I listen to intention: at the first crack of it
Serve the upflowing of a winged horn,
The champing of seeds in the Bull's mouth,

Smell the great flocks of grass.
Nothing is yet fixed:
Among unhooked limbs, parted blebs,
The parcels of last night's carrion
Nothing comes to roost, not even leaves.
Little silences fly about.

Even red is black,
Even night's red is black
Though I taste its first dull burnishing;
Thin black, grey grass, pewter
As a world wakes up its green
So the Bull can walk on it.

Digging at Dawn

Digging at dawn, feeling not seeing the line,
Digging half-blind, alone save for slither –
Birds glued by fog into trees,
Hearing my breath propounding the fog

Knowing, if I shout, if a stone now ring
Or I strike two hands like a lantern
Birds will sing, here, head-high
Perched about this cloud in their labyrinth

But now sleep on,
I had rather be digging at dawn
Watching the dirt thicken
Than walking on pavements

Among all the roosting lungs
The ten million coal-feathered lungs
Whose breath has exhausted the birds,
Walking or sleeping still

Walking or waking
Underneath rooms,
Trapped by their dreams
Against the dark meat of her skyline.

Altitude

In these hills the sky is close to me,
Coming between trees at its own pace,
Going its own way, going when cloudy the wind's way
Which is also its way, but always very close

Say at most a buzzard high and more generally
Down on the stoop of the hill, down
On the goat god's horn which hides
Among fig and prickle, down with the falling leaf.

When it builds itself towers they are little towers,
Towers of rain, or more terribly towers of emptiness,
Collapses of unseen glass, puddles of wind
In their panes so I wince out for signs

As I touch to the buds of clouds, which are brailled in dew
Or cold on the head like cobbles
When I walk on the walking stones in a porridge of sleet
To a heaven about man-high, and close, ah so very close.

And over my sky there's a bigger sky,
Wider than fields, taller than Canegou,
Disdaining its mind though subject to dawn
And any such solar occasion: this I am thankful for

A sky and a sky and an outside sky,
The last smooth rind on the pip and beyond
The planets I walk in my pendulum,
The gap of the unforming fathom, the hollow star.

But the sky in these hills winding close to me
Turns tighter than clocks and so close to me
That tiring of harvests of flesh, staled by the stones
And fearing the grass in its savagery, I hear it is close.

Paco

Welcome to Slot Nose, the walking grunt
With brass ring through freckles and hairy breath,
A large lard poundage, surprising muscles
(He leaves root-digging and even rock-haulage
To the flap-eared shrillness of his seven wives):

Through a barbed fence of cable he appears even friendly,
Lets you scratch his nose and has not yet taken
Fingers in the mouth like a white bunch of worms,
Though he sees the youngest farm-child a suitable morsel
And will eat her one day when wine turns our backs.

But each to his ethic: he gnaws his own children
Given half a chance, by the rubber mouthful.
His wives can't stop him, even seven to one
As he pops their bloated condoms to appealing squeaks,
Spilling scented blood till the sows grow restless.

So in general he's propped away from birth,
All the early stuff of growing. The dug-time
And smug-time of parenthood is nowise for him;
He watches through a wire until his seven brood
Grow too big to eat, and mumbles on the joke: some will be
                                        female

And the green-backed males will be eaten by others.
There's a sawlike screaming at the butcher's down the hill
With a pignote on Monday. The hot drift of blood
Recalls the nearer taste of annihilated broods:
He sniffs his exemption, anxiously wise

And files away fear till the day of his death.
Someone will stalk him with a solid-shotted gun
Because boars have their memories; the pink ugly eye
Holds a bushel of intelligence, and just to see the cart
Will turn him predictably man-mashing mad.

On the Diet of Pigs

Acorns are well known. A wise man
Uses pigs' feet cheaper than a plough:
It only takes the sowing, according to Cato
Remembered by books as that kind of wise.

Nowadays we forget his sweeter simplicities
Like what bait to sow – I'll still say acorns,
Acorns or mast or honey-dipped worms,
Worms steeped in wine amid barrelled chestnut.

Or try live chicks: when I was seven I saw a fat sow
Walk behind a hen with nine brisk chicks
And gobble them up (the farmer boxed my ears
For paying no attention while taking an interest).

If it's true that pigs ate that woman in the newspaper
I don't give a dam. I've often eaten women
From a newspaper myself, licked them right up
And all the white fish that's been wrapped in their thighs.

La Chase

Sitting indoors, hearing the wind
But watching the glass climb,
Buds crawl from the twig and shake into wasps,
I know it's a new not another time,
That the tree breaks its foot
From a passed dimension
In which birds who build nests with straw
Built nests without straw,
In which doves could not clap their wing.

I listen for shots. La Chase
Is months to begin
But begins. If rabbits
Fall from the air or boar
Go fish-faced plummeting
To rummage up flesh
From the pond's pasture
This year is no great matter.
Huntsmen tell taller tales,
Can show you an angel's fall
From a single feather,
Can read you a metre of fish
From a fingerscale.
There is one on the hill
Who three months on
When the pot begins
Will shoot you a wasp
And your cat and his dog and an idiot son.
Three months on
When the Chase begins
This year the chase
Will be months begun:

They are hunting men,
Motorcycle men like rabbits in goggles
Who lie blown open
To twitch and dribble on the verge
In what farmers call
A myxomatosis of lead.

They are hunting the hunters in goggles,
The sky is spinning with wings.
By that bridge in the Corbières
Prefiguring the vines
There are tributes woven in rings;
There are birds nailed up on a cross,
There are angels' wings.
Someone has shot down a someone has shot down a wreath,
Someone has poured out the wine
And the red blood sings.

Against Black Mountain

On certain hills
You see the dawn at midnight,
Not stood on height
        but factors in the bone;

And on those hills
Though kissing open-mouthed
        and ruffling up the straw
You bite the glacier.

Midnight Goats

Sometimes in the darkness by the light of their breathing
    I have seen a little version of heaven,
I have seen it in the phosphor of their lungs
  at the meadow's edge
    where their eyes soft as blood
    seem livers of shadow
to drip among the waters of the leaves
as now with the brain burst open
the skull blades shine.

They stand in a turning of the moon with their head full of
                            candles
and root their hoofs in wax.
I hear their hiss of breath, their
heat inside the silence, as they mouth out little cobbles to the
                            moon,
their causeway into night. They utter
      shiny ribbons in the branches, a frosting
fleeced in bubbles on which their nostril shells
go tinselling like snails;
          and then
head upwards first and afterwards head only
they glide their horns and float.

A doe-goat in the zenith-time is head, all head:
 the stations of the eyes, the feather-frisk of ear,
a tooth ticked like a rosemary –
 the rest is only shade, a dewy disembodiment of thistle.
I sense one planting hoofs
 but only hear my heart; the heads now flock about
and yet I feel no footfall, just a thudding in the wrist,
a certain palpitation as
 the male heads
 glide hill high through labyrinths of horn
 like eagles from the cwm.

This flight is what I prize,
This after midnight minute
 of magicking about
when beasts leaf off their hooves
 to soar horizon high
and gossip in their angelling.
It's then that all things rise,
 the dead ones in the hill,
 the juiceless genealogies,
 while trees unfix their will
and stones come inches out.

Fruit

The curé ate honey, ate wheat bread then cheese,
Disdained greasy meat to the last sausage,
Saying flesh is not animal fruit
Anymore than the bough is the apple.
A man eats the apple, not plunders the bough,
So with meat: let meat eat the grass,
Sip up hay, the garrigue's salty shoots,
Then let it give fruit, little dungs
Little firstlings or truffles.
He waxed about horse turds like apples,
Foxes like pips, and the goats with their grape
Saying let these things grow into corn,
Let them flavour the vine,
Let them flow: I will sip;
Let them give back their fruit as may be,
Apple or grape or else pip.
I will drink up the wine in its season
Out of cups like the woman's hole
(Did he jest, five rims at the table like wounds?)
Disdaining his water, eating no meat and no fish.

Berunguela the Good, and Blanche come out of Castile,
Both of them came this way, a procession of dust at the time
Jaunting from water to well, from well unto watering place:
Both of them sisters, both of them mothers of saints,
Saints from the beds of Kings, whose God preferred carpenters.

Breathing at Night

Breathing at night, I hear this other breath,
Stop breathing, but this breath goes on,
So ponder: is it my ghost, an old ancestral lung,
Death's annotated self, or is my flesh of grass
Already straw?
                    Breathing at night,
Returning into breath, accepting doubleness
I let the young world breathe me, dark and light:
Unpeeling spectres, sparkle on the stone;
Down in the field I am the breath of mint,
I breathe out stars and then become their milk,
Breathing at night.
                    Breathing myself,
I am the goat and horse,
The widow in her shawl,
The snaker with his stick,
A wise man bagging snails before his sun is up,
The idiot divining daffodils.
The Goths lie out and rustle in my breath.
I breathe the well-kempt hillside and the rummage of the bull.

And knowing this, I breathe into the hill,
I blow upon the stone and fossils crawl
Snail backed on shelves of midnight.
I breathe out eider on my eiderdown.

Breathing at night, I breathe but not to kiss.
I breathe out gnats and crabs, and then the salt of frost.
I hear you breathe my breath. You are my breath.
I breathe the bones that make you
And uncoil from lungs your nerves,
Your little curl of veins, then breathe your breath of apple,
Your maggot breath, and then your breath of wasps.
Breathing the night at night,
                              inside my cage of bones
A stream explodes the hill,
A snail lets out the sun,
The midnight lake becomes a dish of tortoises.

Silk Hairs

They grew silk hairs at the crotch
And lay down with fabled wives
    whose laps sprouted mink before mink,
Famous long-ago men
Who did not seal letters with wax
    but Castilian silver:
Rodrigo Diaz de los Camberos,
Gonsalve Pedro de Molina,
Gonsalve de Orvanga
    who came to these hills

Whose peasants forgot to eat,
Whose mothers forgot.

They talk even now of Castilian nobility:
Do they mean the nobility of silver,
The chasing of certain blades at Toledo –
Obscene damascening?

I think of the peasant's damascened furrow.
The wind wipes it out. It is history deep
But noble is not a word to apply.
His spit dries falling – shall I call it silver?

The peasant has seeds in his bowels
                          and his sweat
Is a torrent of pips. When he moves
The heartland's in scab; he infects
Every field with a rash of apples,
His step is contagious with vine;
When he claps his disgusting hands it is bread
Or the glittering filth of God's fishes.

Show him a Knight of Castile:
You show him an Inca in smoke,
You show him a myth disembowelled;
He hears the sword sawing iron, the marrow-bone
                          scream in the passes.
Show him himself. He sees himself bleed his own acres,
He hears his pulse fill up with orchards,
His heartbeat shift stone after stone
While those knights in their armour
Do not even bequeath a tin-can.

Pig Killing in Languedoc

At first, killing pigs is a man's business:
Two men to sieze and then one with the knife
While several small dogs watch the squeal drip down
Into sealable jars. Man with the blade
Hot for skinning, the saw lopping logs
From the parent trunk, a tree-axe for splitting:
His skill tricks hides from the boar's coat.
But afterwards it's woman's business, family women
For the intricate marding and high-priced pickling
Of knobcherries, sweetbreads and such prize bits
As remember acorns and the rumour of oaks;
While invited-in friends and those to whom honour is due
Stuff gobbets of tripe into dishes, set
Lesser fat into brine, stack some parts in salt
And string some for smoking: so here there is pork,
Here ham, and there shrivels bacon to a green stick.
The men have all gone to their ritual cleaning,
First the thumb, then the blade, then under
The death tree's wickerwork darkness
Unfastening bottles arterial with wine.
They drink till the pig saints sit on their tongue,
Pig saints and dog saints to nose up their song.
But woman's work goes on until dark
In a non-stop chopping and chuckling
Of afterbirth tales, though long before dusk
The children who never stop laughing
And hooping and whooping and spitting out sick
Take over licking, and eat up the fun.

Marrow

The fire is catching our cold
The logs have got the catarrh
The grate grumbles mouthfuls of steam

The children scream under the door
That the mist is hanging with apples,
Apples on branches of smoke:

We punish them back to the moors.
In the white out, over the moors,
Their wings flap like burning paper.

We hunch, spill time from the tap.
On the shoulderblades of the house
The coldness is piled up in stones.

Knowing goat-movement on a prehistoric upland –
When winds turn the gorse these walk in their wake,
Scrunching on snails and saliva-pickings
Or licking at the belly of a storm
As at drippings of the Billy –
I see no longer rutting and buffing
Nor the buffering hump as two take fifty,
For some become willing wives:
The one with a cyst has been faithful a week
To the buck without horns but the clubbing head.
Often while her sisters run away
She will nibble his loins
With her brash cotton mouth and her tongue of lint.
Her kisses, like her milk, taste of smoky hair.

In the wake of this bearded Queen
Walk my other capricorns, rustling to stall:
Leah and that name not named,
God-Mother Goat by the Maggot Tree
Who waits with three armpits and a lizard's hole.

Thunder has broken the milk, and the windows spider.
A dog barks close to the lake;
                it is spreading ripples
And jarring the glass with its decibels
As if it is coughing out teeth
Save its howl stays whole, is a hole

With a gum full of stars.
               The water
Shrinks back from its lungs. It barks
At its bark on the lake, at its clouding echo
Till the mirror comes out in fur, and the shallows curdle;
Hills freckle with unsparked fire. We are gasping mildew,

And give the storm best, then best
                  like these cats
Turn away from the dish as if they have sipped at a battery
Though elsewhere, out on the lake
Men crouch beside lowered masts
And pull in their pots and lines
Then plug a fresh cast astern,
              for fish still rise
Mistaking the thunder's flash and snapping at rods of light.

Goats on Black Mountain

It's the Sunday of rut, so we watch with wine
While two bucking billies slip among the goats
To make wives out of daughters and breed new wives,
Ourselves protected by the tingle of a fence

From the juiced-up jerking of the bouncing billy
There prancing to horn. Their two clenched lumps
Outfist even boar, bear, ram or lowland bull
And they carry, like a rattler, extra sex in the head,

Two buried sweets by the horn, two acorns,
Lime sticky acorns they will blot on your sleeve.
These for several weeks in a sacerdotal hunch
The two bucks have pissed on, for themselves and each other

To give a milky must, sallowing the nostril,
Fogging the whims of their quarter-sized daughters
Whose tails lift in heat . . .
                              gobble walnuts of dung,
Snuffle chalorous juice as a zest, and begin.

It takes about a minute each goat at the first
To poke out a maidenhead ripened since Spring:
At each quick stab of the bloodred arrow
The locals applaud in a fresh glass of wine,

The men with a scoff, the women
With sidelong delicate contempt for the men
Who couldn't if they tried and wouldn't even try.
Then the bucks grow cunning: they'll be here a month

Running with the flock, ploughing all eighty
So they've time for a jest, like knackering each other
With a yeasty ram amidships on a planted back.
They dismount to tangle horns while the nannies eat grass,

Growing canny in turn. Some, smaller than dogs,
Object to being mounted by a thorn-headed horse
In a frenzy of beard; so they learn how to sidle
On the axle of a tree so he can't cock a leg.

Once the rutting cools, the locals depart
And the herd settles down, moving now to crop
Or skit away from shadows in a quick glance of wind,
Some to play at virgins, some at being Queen:

One whiter than the rest, with a glittering cyst,
Has kept Hornless Billy for three whole weeks,
Ruling other wives, touching lip and tongue
To the berries of his head, the burrs of his loin.

A hogshead deep in wine, I remember that Book
Whose Magicians enter flocks to graze the banks of Time;
So looking at these so separate from those,
She guarding his flanks with her cyst and horn,

I wonder: what hide did they choose?
Was it goats, these goats, in eternal rut
That great pair chose for their fabled marriage,
That mad midnight Sheba and her noon-hard Solomon?

[89]

Love Poem South

I lie with your hands eating me
Your fingers like worms eating me
As once when I lay in a dream
By a broken grave

So now in the hammock of your breath
Where I listen to stones to bedbones creaking

And then the primal typhoon
Driving land into ridges
Leave its last slurry at here,
Drop hutch after hutch of granite

Then dry off into a star
A coal-bright ascending spiral

Seeing what goats, seeing what pigs, seeing what horses chew:
Horses the grass to a blunt bristle,
Goats eating shoot, pigs into root, picking up trees by the handle,
Grubbing up worlds by the stone, unlidding the fire;

Seeing what snails, seeing what beetles chew,
And – peeling the bole – the weevil under the bark
Slivering silver caves, the sprung-open clockwork of ants,
Seeing what these chew, wood to a web's spectre,
Cocoons of nails, the spiderbag gutsing the cone;

Seeing what dogs, seeing what apes, seeing what mice chew:
One thing first then another till at last they unmask the mind,
Seeing what brains, seeing what eyes, seeing what loins chew
All at the pump of love in its shade of lungs,
Scoffing rib after rib after rib as girls snap teeth from a comb;

Seeing what men, seeing what winds, seeing what Gods chew,
Blood, waxflame and prayer, the swilling cannibals of rot;
Seeing what these, seeing what all things chew
I meet at this butcher's stump
The bee that is guzzling orchards,
The worm with your child in its mouth.

Flat Rain

Flat rain, of course, is a different rain,
I mean rain on the flat lands, rain on the fat
Of a pond perhaps larded with carp –
That rain hissing. Or rain on the tarmac sea:

It's a vertical rain, or more generally downfalling rain
(Not to be confused with the water or crusted glass
Thrown from the tops of waves and sometimes rising,
Sheeting or otherwise fusing) since

Only in mountains can the rain fall up,
Spraying from a fellside under your cape
Or cocking a wing to straddle a ridge
Which is also a margin, and bomb

From some lower cloud a whole lakeful up
From the beak of nothing. Here there is sun
And yourself stood higher than God in a dry blue sky
Then a slime takes hold of your trouserleg, a whirlpool

Spumes from the rock and you teeter there upon parable
Borne out of paradox: one little cwm
Opening its lips and giving an upward gobful
In parabolas of light; but I come to digress

What with seas and mountains from flatland rain
About which is nothing but rain. In short
Which is falling water. What varies is height,
The height of the land, the pitch of the cloud,

The distance of heaven from victim, or God
From the blistering grace in which green things flow
And which brings out the snail till it drowns in it:
A rain in which trees are alone in their ease

While rivers waddle on, growing sternly obese.

Cura Pastoralis

The Curé said
When you lie with a woman
You think about woman

When you lie with yourself
You think about the world

And then, with practice,
Think about God,

God in his heaven,
His heaven his world
But hardly his woman

Or not many women.

Old monsieur shall I call him Dubois
Dropping mousedirt from his nose
Peanuts from his ears
Unbuttons his parsnip
With the news on his knees
Like an old maid's skirt,
Sits there reading his knees
Making paper darts from his skirt,
And a complex origami from the radix of his tease

And his brother who is Mayor
And his sister who is Mayor
And his father who is Mayor
Whichever is Mayor
Does not care

That monsieur Dubois
Might break through *La Dépêche* or *La Terre,*
The column through the column,
The column quaintly carping
Then the column with its curls,
And affright our little girls

Since the said little girls
See the stallion in the meadow
The goat upon the hill,
Have dabbled with the skeleton
And heard a dirty chuckle in the bough,
Have even seen some of them
Adders and long-legged lightnings mate

And the commune will conspire
The demise of this Dubois
Before our rising lovelies
Need to read or light a fire.

The Red-Eyed Rat

Threading my inchy sleep
You rat down your sootbeam,
Bone-faced with stars. Their milk
In all windows bleeds. I
Startle awake. You have ruffled my house,

Now, like a monkey, wise,
Full-bellied on dream
Sit buddharing over the clock
In the warm of its tick, just
Glassing a smile. So your teeth crackle.

I talk by the stars.
I long to talk to you, Rat.
I talk by a dim lamp.
You listen but will not speak.
You have heard me before, perhaps

In our last life. When I talk
I am inedible. Breath
Makes us inedible
Or at least to a single rat.
You have listened to too much meat,

Would prefer men dead
And then slim them a bit.
Yet I wake: you are not surprised,
You have time, a will to be sociable,
Perhaps only come when I'm here

When the family is here,
For a wry look, or a gulp of our prayer
Or just to be seen,
Being only seen
By me, by the family.

I listen. You come to exist
Wall-high in a faint scuff.
I look. You have substance there.
We look. You sit solider,
Striking your fire from that look.

I speak. You lodge into time.
We speak. You take on our mass,
Pressure the clock
Which rocks as you disappear.
I have thrown my first boot

So you run, climb off into stars
More real now than real
Though invisible.
You need even now to be seen
Because I do not think God sees you,

Does not look well on his rats,
Has no need to see them in place
Or to number them with his sparrow.
May listen far off to your wit
But not share a table with it:

The corpse is not God's meat.
I long to talk to you, rat.

Goat Self and God Self

I batten on milk,
Sucking the teat of a cloud,
Some fleshy lump in the air
Doing me daisies down:

So also the baby goats
Hang from their mother shag
To whiten the earth of their gum
Becoming, like me, of age

To chew little chunks of stars
Or nibble in loony space
Juice from the moon's thistle
And pretend we are God's alone.

Snake in Particular

Stark in its coil of veins
Snake unbubbled its wisdom,
Oiling its words,
Keeping its silence moist
On the in-and-out fur of its tongue
As it moved ahead of its utterances,
Breathing like grass.

Yet watching it pass
I did not see this
But a length of indifference
Trawling a long tube of hunger.
Seductive patterer:
I forgot about Eve
And struck several times to kill
Being practised to miss.

Pigeons in Winter

Bigger than trees
bulb out of poles
ballooning God's rumour in a rummage of wings

        days the wind rattles
        the windowframe sky

        days when tomorrow
        falls off its sashes

Fatty confirms
with his beakful of Word.

Days of light airs
when they flap
        doodle-footed
close to my mind
taking the biscuit

Fatty stays slim

        days of big bluster
        days of intention
when pigeons explode

Fatty buds up again
preening his incense
green in his plumpness like
          boldly branched apple
dapper Tibetan
and slily white-waxing
his ready-sliced nimble
red cabbage feet.

Since they answer to any spell
My typing calls up goats:
Shift of key, clack clack, little bell
The hillside is morning bare
With the herd in the beard of a cloud
Or crumbling through the garrigue,
So I tap and they straggle here
In a half-mile chain down the hill
Rattling their horns, ringing electric wire
Shift of key, clack clack, little bell

Some say that seven-foot Pierre
Draws them in and out of his mind:
I know real goats unreel
When my typewriter yattering keys
Calls them to give men milk
Shift of key, clack clack, little bell
Calls them to pizzle in pails
Goatish moons in puddles of froth
Cloud-tasting and sticky like snails.

Shift of key, clack clack, little bell
When night cramps my fingering bones
And my words queue nose to tail
Does the herd eat the moonlight hill
Or congeal in its crown of stones,
Congeal and become the stones
And the damps that the stones conceal?

Shift of key, clack clack, little bell
All things become what they are:
As they crop your shadow, Pierre,
They are your dream made real
And doubled again in me,
Grave herds that moon in the head
In a landscape bristling with words.
The typewriter's out-of-doors,
A star's weight pressing each key
Dewfall trembles its bell
And the bells of the ruminant herds
Shift of key, clack clack, little spell.

Magic Numbers

Three stones on a jam and butter,
Three slimy plumtree pips:
One dripped on your laundered cloth,
One fouled my politest trousers,
One snapped a tooth at the root:
Who says there's no magic in numbers
Or only joy in the plum?

Four billygoats in a stormcloud
Eating a fig tree's hair:
One broke his horn on an axle,
One splintered himself in a fall
And went off to lowland slavery
Arthritic and slack in will.
Now two have service of ninety
Or one against one must fight:
Who says there's no magic in numbers
Or only zest in the male?

Two serpents mating at sunset
In oviviviparous curl
Siezed on the self same lizard
Too high for the trick of its tail:
The male ate the better supper,
The female ate all of the male
And choked on her three-bellied banquet:
Who says there's no magic in numbers
Or only harm in the toad?

Now you by the oblong water
Which tilts so will not square
Yourself and long-legged image
In which connections blear:
The triangle thrown by a rafter
Turns diamond in the pool,
The plumtree smells like a viper,
The goat breeze rises sour
Around my well-rinsed britches
Which wince where their tooth is drawn
But you are tricked by a poem
And trapped in its numbers here:
Who says there's no magic in numbers
Or only trousers pair?

To Dig in the Morning Sun

To dig in the morning sun
Between coffee and wine
Is better than kissing

A truth independent of backs
Independent of spades
The quality of coffee
The quantity of wine

And sometimes of kissing.

Another Digging

A brick soil. Only winds will break it,
Winds or else worms, or a sly root.
Man will not break it, nor beast's foot:
It will break men, and the beast bends
Stubbing the hole in the hoof, burning the nerve.
When a horse comes down it will lie in splinters.
It will break men, so let the sun burn
The rains win its heart with a soft tickle
And pray for a midwinter sog
Or that coldweather mountainous God
Of the Cathars in prayer
To bear down the sky in a harness of prickle,
Then sprinkle your seed in a booted walk.
Each day continue your walk
Picking it free of the snail,
And listen for roots to explode,
The vine to winch out a flint
Or the radish to crater . . .

I look at these soils. They lie in my last year's turning
Exact as they were, as they are. They are mine.
I could build them into a tower or cobble a well.
Their world is my well, my tower. It steepens with time.

Wind Scale

I'll count every wind now the sky's rolling South:
How one sparks with gnats to burn on your arm,
How one's full of magnets tugging out hair
Or unseating corn, and one splits the plane trees
To pillage their colours, or pines for their ullage
So night smells of casks.

                       There's a green wind, of course,
To slither down hills and smother the dust
In a topcoat of dribble. When grit chuckles back
There's a brother to drown it in slime for a month
Then float all the grasses dark side up. Over bristly peaks
Wait six winds of black to seacoal the sunset
To damper flame, snail dawn in silver,
Slag winds and cinder winds tasting of heat –
Some made by light in the lens of a mountain
And some born of fumeroles in volcanic tuff.
Earth winds and sea winds and sun winds I can take,
But I'll not count the one that chatters fools' teeth
In their cells at Toulouse or Montpelier Asylum
Since that one's a bully to madmen and drunks;
Besides, there's a friend roving free who is stronger
To turn peasants mad (if he finds one sober)
And send their girls treading the grapejuice from a snake
Or kicking out skulls from a backbone of flint:
So, yes, I'll count this one and the small one that sits
In the beak of an eagle and guides it into sheep,
But the thermals rising from flocks I'll not count,
Nor bellows nor oxen rapped in the gut.
I must meet the cold eye and suffer my preference
For one to empty sows both of piglets and milk
For one to peel time like bark off of lepers

For one to skin trees without scattering flowers
And drive away lupus in a squadron of rats . . .
I feel a sweet terror when that one blows:
Do I conjure it myself with rocks in its claws
Or does that old ghost in the Charnel at Charenton
With its cancelled-out germs and eclectic molecules?
Is the gap still unclosed in the Father's head?

Tree Snake

When I think of tree's meat, and certainly
Trees have meat for those who have made
The axe blade bleed in them or sucked out their heart
At a sucked boles thumb, I never think

Cow's meat, man's meat, or even
Dog's within dogwood or a the high-horned goat:
No, tree's meat is snake's meat, is venom dripping
On the fire's balsam, is the black-ash writhers

Wreathing their whispers in the smoke's afterbirth;
Such snakes as udder cows or enter
Or fall from the woman's hole are tree's meat
And thereby spit leaves, hiss berries and strike out sparks.

In lowland winter, mud prints its oak-snake
When adders sleep, in a scaly rustle;
And on rowan heights taller than flesh, coil fancies:
Among crags of thorn the original Wyrm

So sometimes, stepping through Myth, a man needs warm
His five limbs to the marrow's echo.
                              Then this
With its grey hood inflated, its flickering tongue,
Is the Great Snake for ever cullioned in ash.

Black Mountain Boar

Sometimes, in summer pines above Saissac,
There or in bracken sweaty with noon,
The eye stops on dropped posts, dolmen
Or grey humps of upland marble

Which move among small pig grunts;
One or two move, always with grunts
Neither anxious nor certain. And pigs, you think,
Striding to glimpse out a sow, and even

With squashed mushroom ears and peg-ended feet
A hulling balloon castored by piglets –
But beware: these are boar, Black Mountain Boar
Unsure on the tusk but each with a hard wedge bite

For the cake of your thigh. Terrible to see
The pine-needles rusted to iodine,
The rock turned wax with your crumbs
While green backs, rashering the blubbery noon,

Mowl up with eyes as empty as nostrils
To drink a whole man through the nose.
There are silences here where a scream disappears:
Were these bubbles toadstools, a circlet of children?

The posts stop moving, the turf without grunts
Hardens its back in the pines above Saissac.
The dream goes back into tins; six huntsmen
Come spectering past with guns on their shoulders

Or rise from the tomb of a car. They seek –
As they sought – the last barbed nest of young piglets
Throating their bristling stockade, still tuskless
With old man's salt on the bark of their tongue.

The Man in the Mill

for Yves Vidal

Down by his mill in a cleft
He is gardening snakes. He's an expert
On snakes, snakes and fish, and the way water curls
Through a mill's dank verticals
Spinning on slats in a spit's froth
Or wreaths round the hub of a race.
On fish he is good; on snakes almost pure
(Having brailled them by hand then traced them through books);
On water a cool-eyed philosopher
Learning with Leonardo you have only to look
To unbutton it molecule by molecule.
On water, in the end, I trust him most.
I trust him on water like I trust his dog.

He tells me, throwing for his dog,
How vipers swim here in head-heavy swim.
I have not seen such a swim, and yet I believe him:
He believes in himself. And how vipers,
Vipers not greensnakes, lie
Ten feet down in the pool where we dive
Until fish eat them.
                                      'Pike,' I reply
Watching a depth-drowsy tyre-tube swallow its ends.
'No, not pike.' His spit, plug-yellow,
Venoms the earth. His spit is like piss.
'You will not believe me: I've seen a sand-viper
 Lie perfectly still and be eaten by trout,
 Trout not pike, a dangerous snake.
 You will not believe me.'

[115]

I do not believe him.
He believes in himself. I walk to the fall
Whose waters compress in a black churdle,
Hurling syllable down after syllable
Till here for a second there is more to the inch,
More water, more sound of water,
The pulse of time packing in
Then slackening, perming to froth;
And learning through him from Leonardo how to look
I can see before the softness of froth
Its weight gristle down from the hill,
Black water, thicker than liquorice
(Emblem of one kind of lie). I see no snakes,
I see no fish. I see no fish eat a snake
Or snake eat a fish. In my time
I've seen rats at a snake numbed by cold
That otherwise would have vacuumed them,
And a grasssnake bitten by ants;
But here, in this water?

Well, the pool is a place for Myth;
From the leafy flicker of an eye
The gumble of the mill
Makes a miracle of eyewash
And eyewash again from the miracle
Since six local families drink it
Before it suds down the hill.
There's a town forked under the ravine
Whose waterworks pump it back
Through a long vibration of hose
To this purified factual tap.

Seeking the slier drink
I turn its brass-bellied faucet:
A snake dribbles down from its lip
Like liquid under my hand
To flow through his garden of snakes
Past the marrow-beds and cucumber
One of nine cool breeds of *couleuvre,*
(A greensnake, vipers can't climb
Any more than they're happy to swim).
I tell where his snake has come
To hose up a little water
From the leaking teat of the tap,
Quote tall American books
About lie-snakes hugging an udder
To plug it empty of milk.
He doesn't believe me, though,
The Man with Snakes in his Garden.
Or perhaps it was mating shade,
Saw the pipe as a twin or lover
And felt a relating pulse
In its dribbling sibilances . . .
He scarcely believes me still,
The Man with Snakes in his Garden,
The Expert shy of the Poet?
Uncorks an anis instead,
Soiling clean water to milk,
Pool water, rinsed in the pool:
'Our truths drink together,' he says.

Will the Lie lie drunk with the Liar?

Tonight

As herds beneath the pull of the hill
    Fall from four legs down and sleep,
Birds die like snowflakes and the gull
    Drops inland with a salted beak,
And fish, secure from bore or rip,
Hang under boughs their fruit:

I look across ten miles of night
    And suck the shadow from my thumbs
Then think of simple answers, not
    The subtleties that pleased me once:
The silence bristling like a dog
Suggests a much less abstract God

Than that sidereal benign
    Unwhiskery old anthromorph
Ignoring every suppliant line
    Buzzed from cathedrais in the north.
I sense a howling gothic mask
Buried in nettles, and I itch to ask.